Opposites

Wet and Dry

Siân Smith

Raintree is an imprint of Capstone Global Library Limited, a company incorporated in England and Wales having its registered office at 7 Pilgrim Street, London, EC4V 6LB – Registered company number: 6695582

www.raintreepublishers.co.uk
myorders@raintreepublishers.co.uk

Text © Capstone Global Library Limited 2015
First published in hardback in 2014
The moral rights of the proprietor have been asserted.

Edited by Brynn Baker
Designed by Peggie Carley
Production by Victoria Fitzgerald
Originated by Capstone Global Library Ltd
Printed and bound in China

ISBN 978 1 406 28305 1
18 17 16 15 14
10 9 8 7 6 5 4 3 2 1

British Library Cataloguing in Publication Data
A full catalogue record for this book is available from the British Library.

Acknowledgements
We would like to thank the following for permission to reproduce photographs: Alamy: milos luzanin, 14; Getty Images: ballyscanlon, 5, 22a, Dave King, 13, lina, aidukaite, 8, NI QIN, 10; Shutterstock: A_Belov, 16, Africa Studio, 17, Chamille White, 21 left, drpnncpptak, 9, Ijansempoi, 21 right, Irantzu Arbaizagoitia, 6, back cover bottom, Jjustas, 18, Kemeo, 20 left, Milos Luzanin, 12, restyler, 20 right, Sretnaz, 4, 22b, back cover top.

Cover photographs reproduced with permission of Shutterstock: Aleksandar Mijatovic (right), dinadesign (left).

Every effort has been made to contact copyright holders of material reproduced in this book. Any omissions will be rectified in subsequent printings if notice is given to the publisher.

Contents

Wet and dry

Water is **wet**.

Sand is **dry**.

Milk is wet.

This bed is dry.

The boy is wet.

Now he is dry.

Is this boy wet or dry?

The boy is wet!

The girl is wet.

Now she is dry.

Is this girl wet or dry?

The girl is dry.

The dog is wet.

Now it is dry.

Is this dog wet or dry?

The dog is wet!

Wet and dry quiz

Which of these things are wet?

Which of these things are dry?

Answers on page 22

Picture glossary

dry free from moisture

wet covered with or full of liquid

Index

Answers to questions on pages 20 and 21

The soup is wet.
The towel is dry.

Notes for teachers and parents

BEFORE READING

Building background:

Ask children when they have been wet (bath, swimming pool, rain). How did they get dry?

AFTER READING

Recall and reflection:

Is milk wet or dry? Is sand wet or dry? Can sand ever be wet (talk about the beach)?

Sentence knowledge:

Help children find pages with questions. How do they know? How do they read the sentence if it is a question (rising intonation at the end of the sentence)?

Word knowledge (phonics):

Encourage children to point at the word *wet* on any page. Sound out the three phonemes in the word *w/e/t*. Ask children to sound out each phoneme as they point at the letters and then blend the sounds together to make the word *wet*. Challenge them to say some words that rhyme with *wet* (get, let, met, pet).

Word recognition:

Ask children to point at the word *is* on any page.

AFTER-READING ACTIVITIES

Ask children to soak squares of different materials (cotton, wool, plastic, silk, velvet, felt) in a bucket of water. Then hang up the squares of materials. Which material do they think will dry quickest? Why is there a difference? What would happen if they hung the squares outside in the sunshine?

In this book

Topic

wet and dry

Sentence stems

1. ___ is ___.
2. This ___ is ___.
3. He/She is ___.

High-frequency words

and	or
are	she
he	the
is	these
it	this
now	water
of	which